T0381049

Meet Me Here

Just South of Heaven

Prayer Journal

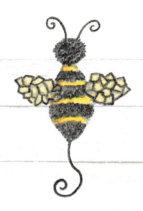

Jill Glorioso

Copyright © 2019 Jill Glorioso.

Interior Image Credit: Jill Glorioso

Cover picture by Madison Pruitt my talented granddaughter.

This book is a work of non-fiction. Unless otherwise noted, the author and the publisher make
no explicit guarantees as to the accuracy of the information contained in this book and in some
cases, names of people and places have been altered to protect their privacy.

All rights reserved. No part of this book may be used or reproduced by any means, graphic, electronic, or mechanical,
including photocopying, recording, taping or by any information storage retrieval system without the written
permission of the author except in the case of brief quotations embodied in critical articles and reviews.

Scripture quotations are taken from the Holy Bible, New Living Translation, copyright ©1996, 2004, 2015 by Tyndale House
Foundation. Used by permission of Tyndale House Publishers, Inc., Carol Stream, Illinois 60188. All rights reserved.

WestBow Press books may be ordered through booksellers or by contacting:

WestBow Press
A Division of Thomas Nelson & Zondervan
1663 Liberty Drive
Bloomington, IN 47403
www.westbowpress.com
1 (866) 928-1240

Because of the dynamic nature of the Internet, any web addresses or links contained in this book may have changed
since publication and may no longer be valid. The views expressed in this work are solely those of the author and do
not necessarily reflect the views of the publisher, and the publisher hereby disclaims any responsibility for them.

Any people depicted in stock imagery provided by Getty Images are models, and
such images are being used for illustrative purposes only.
Certain stock imagery © Getty Images.

ISBN: 978-1-9736-5602-9 (sc)
ISBN: 978-1-9736-5603-6 (e)

Library of Congress Control Number: 2019903048

Print information available on the last page.

WestBow Press rev. date: 4/9/2019

WESTBOW
PRESS*
A DIVISION OF THOMAS NELSON
& ZONDERVAN

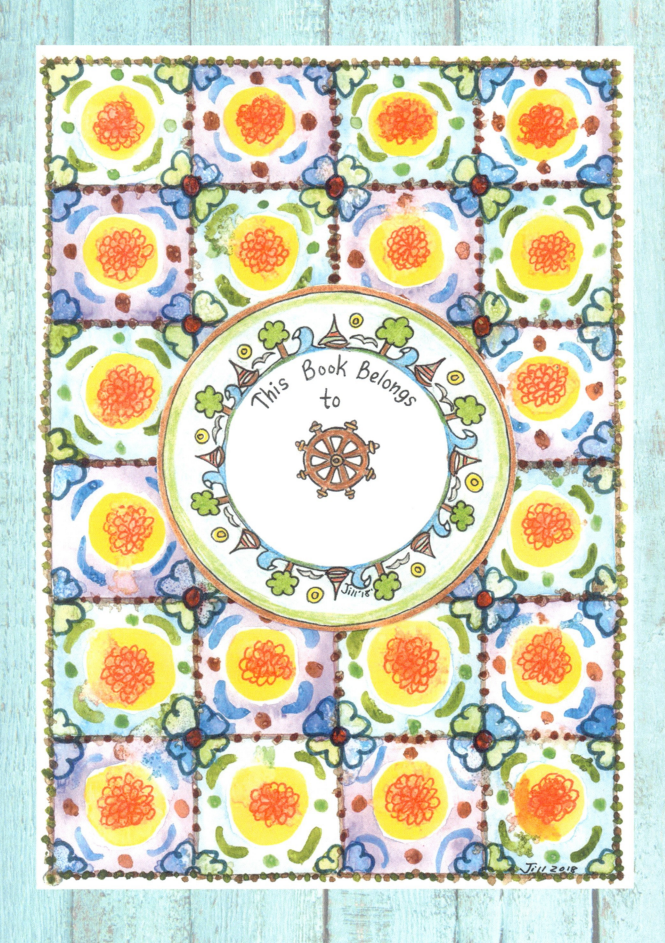

This Book Belongs to

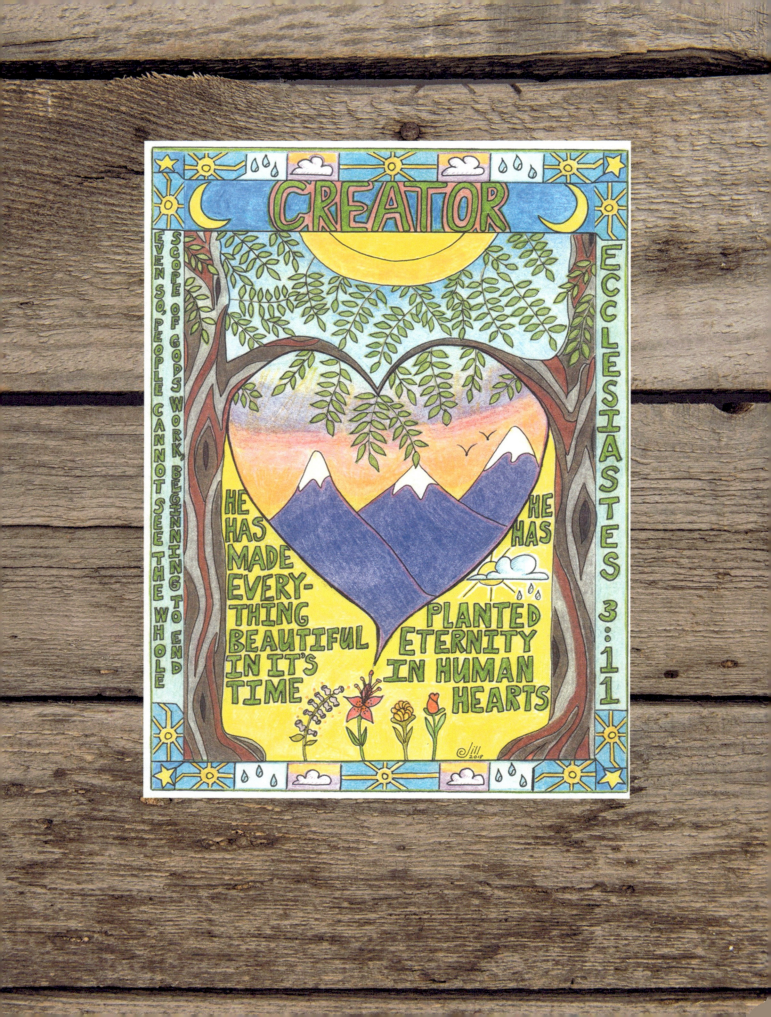

Purpose

The purpose of this book is in hopes that you will take a step and spend time with your Heavenly Father, the one who created you, the one who loves you beyond measure. A few years ago after going to a women's retreat I was convicted to plan on doing something that would take God's help to accomplish. So I decided to journal a morning prayer each day for 1000 days. Originally I planned to journal 1000 days in a row, but once I missed a day I felt guilt and decided that if I missed a day here or there that was okay. Perfection was not my goal, spending time with God was. So every morning I journal one page while having my coffee. It is a set appointment and here I am on day 810. Without God I know this would not have happened.

I will tell you that as time has passed I have found myself in a much closer relationship with Him. Instead of me just figuring He knows my life because He knows everything, I know because I told Him. I have proof, it's in writing. After journaling for many days I also felt convicted to start reading my Bible more; not a devotional but actually the books in the Bible, especially the Gospels. So I started just reading 1 chapter before journaling every day, baby-steps that continue to work for me. As in any healthy relationship, I listen to Him and He listens to me. We are close and I know beyond a shadow of a doubt that He has got my back. He is good, He wants to teach me, He knows I am ready to learn because I come to Him and love Him by spending time with Him. I know that His ways are right and true.

James 4:8 says, "Draw near to God and He will draw near to you." This was written from Jesus' actual brother. Everyones' experience will be a little different because God made us all different.

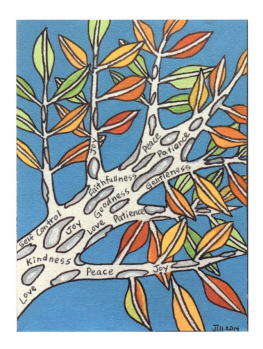

The thing that I hope and pray for you is that you will have a real and close relationship with your Father in Heaven.

One step at a time.

Just make a move

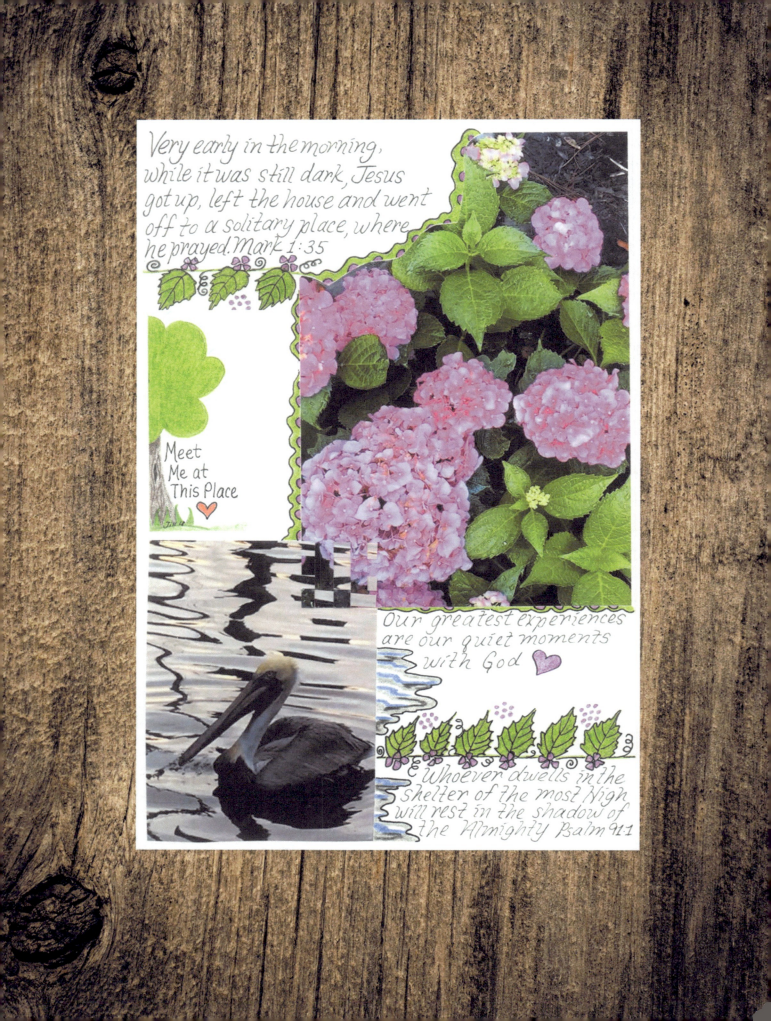

Very early in the morning, while it was still dark, Jesus got up, left the house and went off to a solitary place, where he prayed. Mark 1:35

Meet Me at This Place ♥

Our greatest experiences are our quiet moments with God ♥

Whoever dwells in the shelter of the most High will rest in the shadow of the Almighty Psalm 91:1

Psalm 5:3
Listen to my voice in the morning, Lord.
Each morning I bring my requests to You and
wait expectantly.

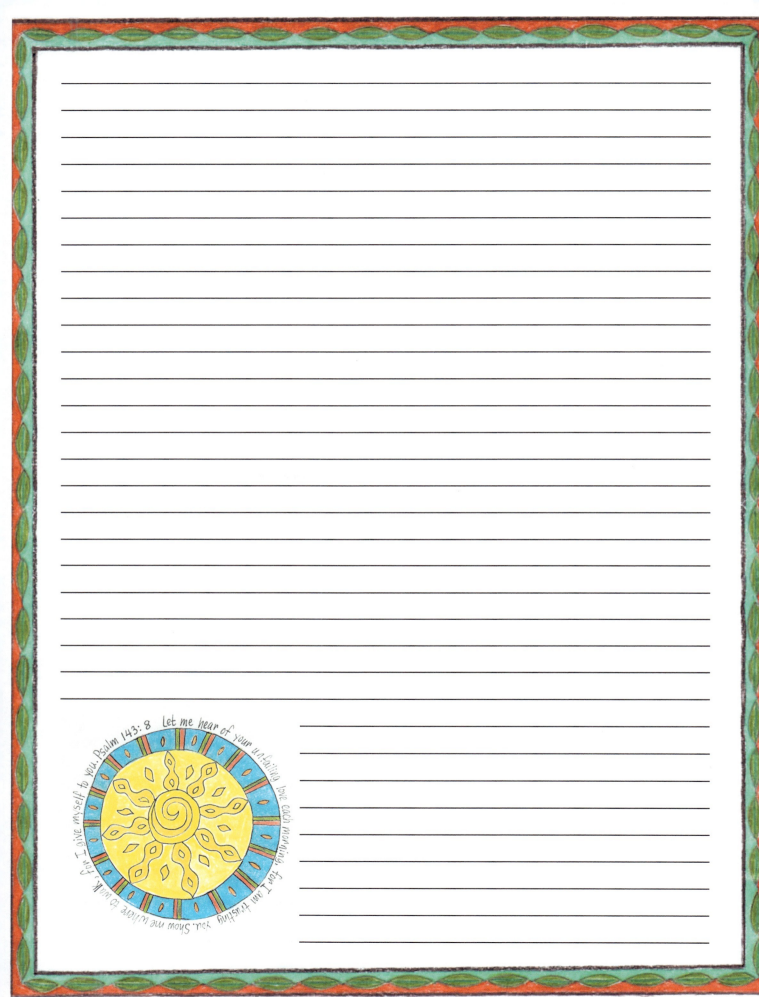

Psalm 143:8   Let me hear of your unfailing love each morning, for I am trusting you. Show me where to walk, for I give myself to you.

_____
_____
_____
_____
_____
_____
_____
_____
_____
_____
_____
_____
_____
_____
_____
_____
_____
_____
_____
_____
_____
_____
_____
_____
_____
_____
_____
_____
_____
_____

I Peter I:6-7

6 So be truly glad. There is wonderful Joy ahead, even though you must endure many trials for a little while. 7 These trials will show that your faith is genuine. It is being tested as fire tests and purifies gold- though your faith is far more precious than mere gold. So when your faith remains strong through many trials, it will bring you much praise and glory and honor on the day when Jesus Christ is revealed to the whole world.

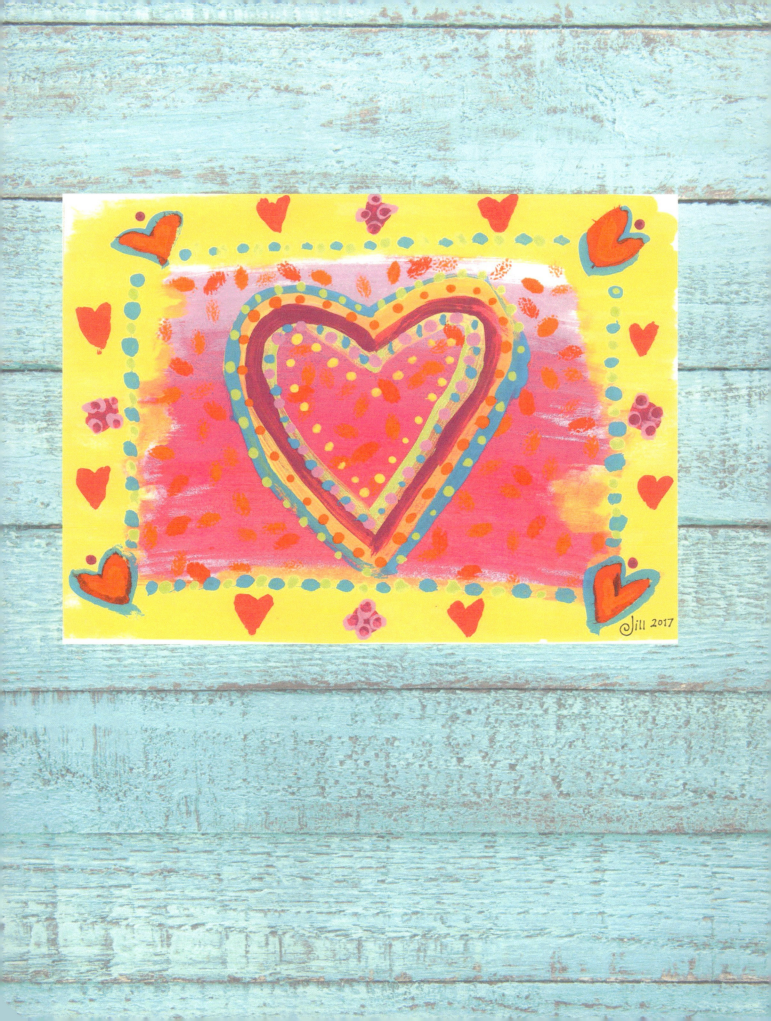

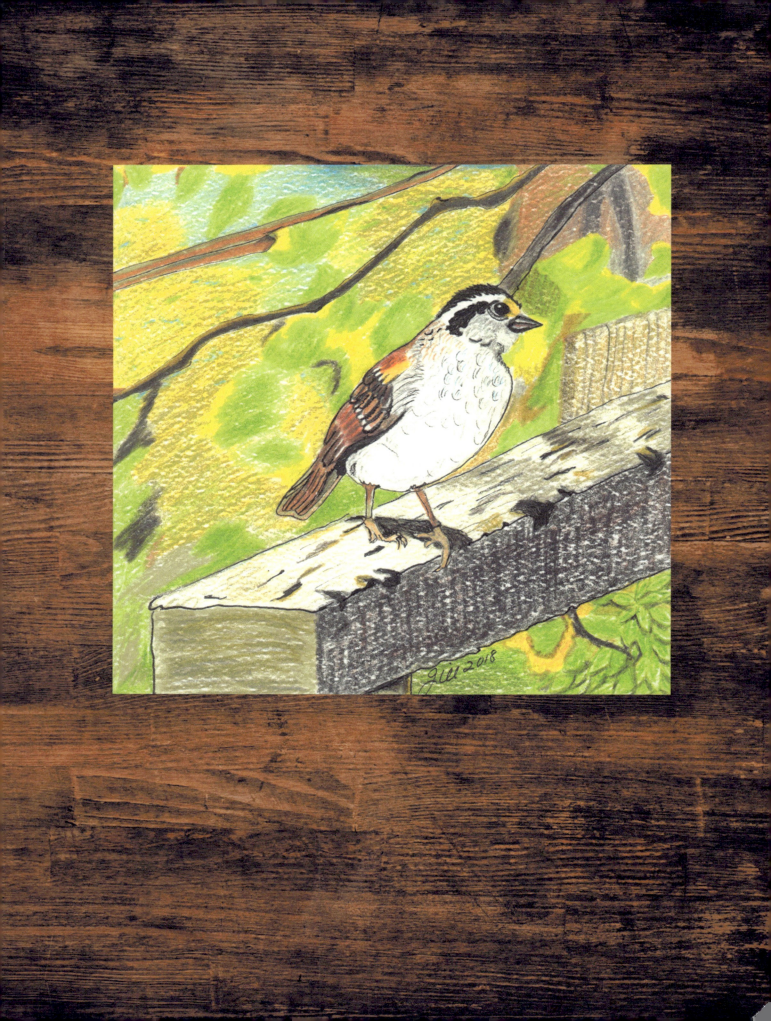

A Free Verse Poem

One

I come to You
Eager to be in Your presence
You smile with JOY
We dance under the tree of life
The birds sing their love song
Over the rocks the waters bubble and tumble
You hold me, understanding my details
Forgiveness is asked for
Forgiveness is given
I sigh with relief
My burdens are lifted
I'm set free
We dance some more
Happy to be together

_____
_____
_____
_____
_____
_____
_____
_____
_____
_____
_____
_____
_____
_____
_____
_____
_____
_____
_____
_____
_____
_____
_____
_____
_____
_____
_____
_____

Colossians 3: 12-14

12 Since God chose you to be the holy people He loves,
you must clothe yourselves with tenderhearted mercy,
kindness, humility, gentleness, and patience. 13 Make
allowance for each other's faults, and forgive anyone
who offends you. Remember, the Lord forgave you, so
you must forgive others. 14 Above all, clothe yourselves
with love, which binds us all together in perfect harmony.

2 Timothy 1:7
For God has not given us a spirit of fear
and timidity, but of power, love and self-discipline.

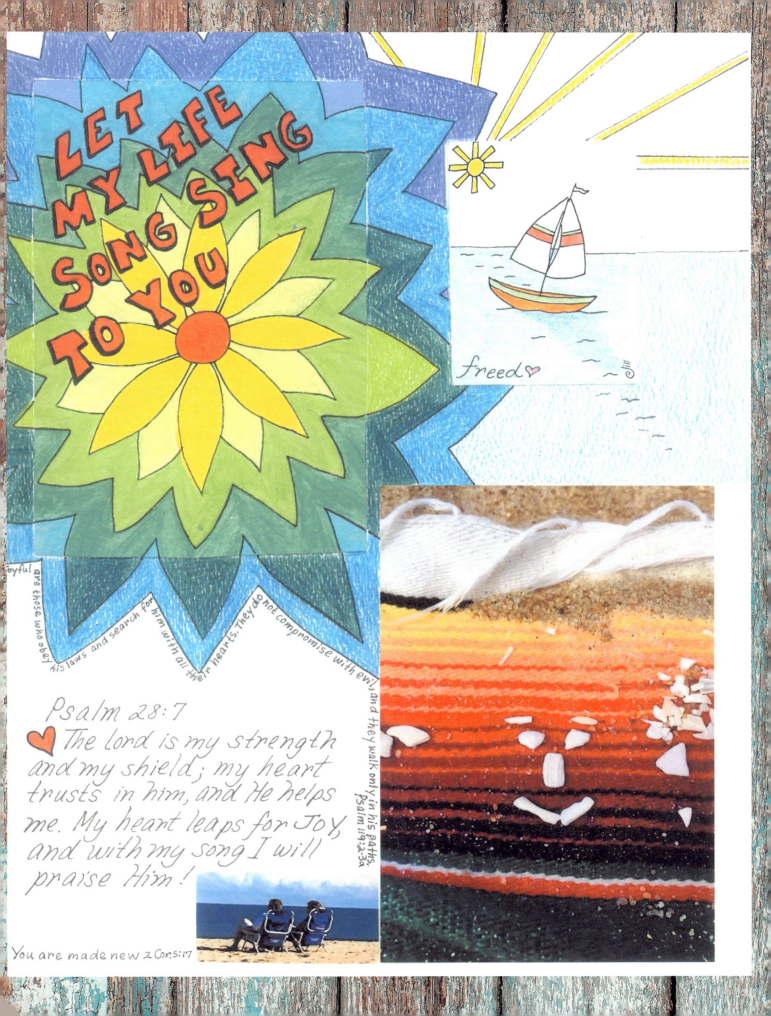

LET MY LIFE SONG SING TO YOU

freed♥ ~Jill

Joyful are those who obey his laws and search for him with all their hearts. They do not compromise with evil, and they walk only in his paths. Psalm 119:2-3a

Psalm 28:7
♥ The lord is my strength and my shield; my heart trusts in him, and He helps me. My heart leaps for JOY, and with my song I will praise Him!

You are made new 2 Cor 5:17

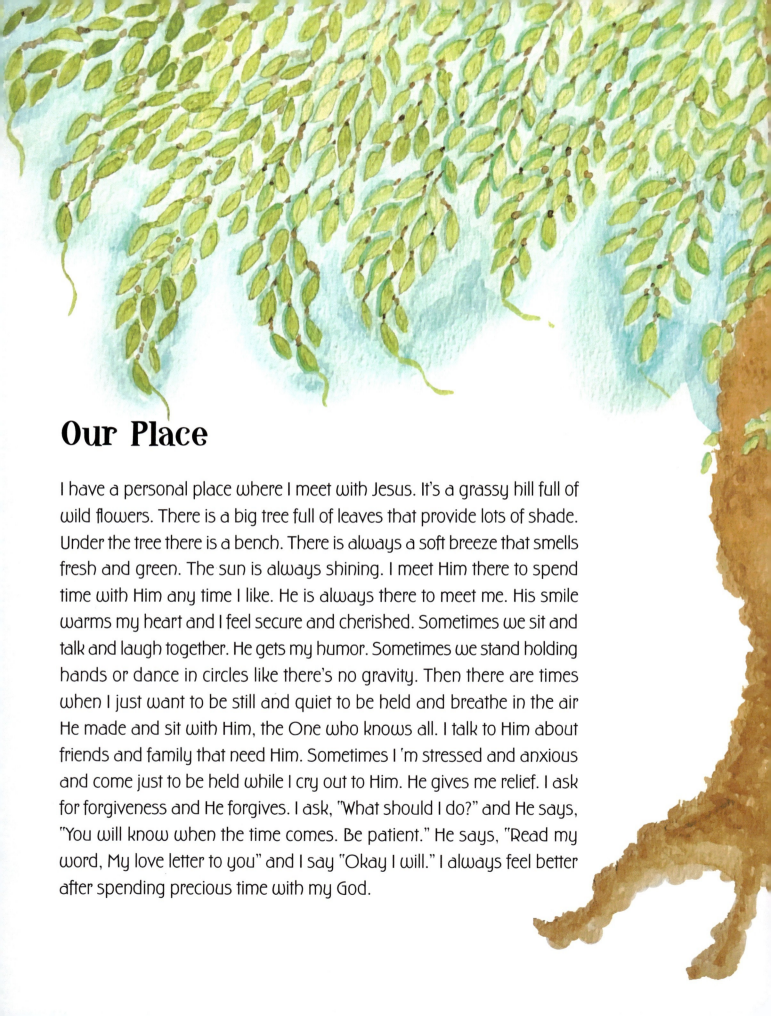

Our Place

I have a personal place where I meet with Jesus. It's a grassy hill full of wild flowers. There is a big tree full of leaves that provide lots of shade. Under the tree there is a bench. There is always a soft breeze that smells fresh and green. The sun is always shining. I meet Him there to spend time with Him any time I like. He is always there to meet me. His smile warms my heart and I feel secure and cherished. Sometimes we sit and talk and laugh together. He gets my humor. Sometimes we stand holding hands or dance in circles like there's no gravity. Then there are times when I just want to be still and quiet to be held and breathe in the air He made and sit with Him, the One who knows all. I talk to Him about friends and family that need Him. Sometimes I'm stressed and anxious and come just to be held while I cry out to Him. He gives me relief. I ask for forgiveness and He forgives. I ask, "What should I do?" and He says, "You will know when the time comes. Be patient." He says, "Read my word, My love letter to you" and I say "Okay I will." I always feel better after spending precious time with my God.

_____
_____
_____
_____
_____
_____
_____
_____
_____
_____
_____
_____
_____
_____
_____
_____
_____
_____
_____
_____
_____
_____
_____
_____
_____
_____
_____
_____
_____
_____
_____

2 Corinthians 3: 15-18

15 Yes, even today when they read Moses' writings their hearts are covered with that veil, and they do not understand. 16 But whenever someone turns to the Lord, the veil is taken away. 17 For the Lord is the Spirit; and wherever the Spirit of the Lord is, there is freedom. 18 So all of us that have had that veil removed can see and reflect the glory of the Lord. And the Lord – who is the Spirit – makes us more and more like Him as we are changed into His glorious image.

_____

_____

_____

_____

_____

_____

_____

_____

_____

_____

_____

_____

_____

_____

_____

_____

_____

_____

_____

_____

_____

_____

_____

_____

_____

_____

_____

_____

_____

_____

2 Peter 1:16-18

16 For we were not making up clever stories when we told you about the powerful coming of our Lord Jesus Christ. We saw his majestic splendor with our own eyes 17 when He received honor and glory from God the Father the voice from the majestic glory of God said to Him, "this is my dearly loved Son, who brings me great JOY." 18 We ourselves heard that voice from Heaven when we were with Him on the holy mountain.

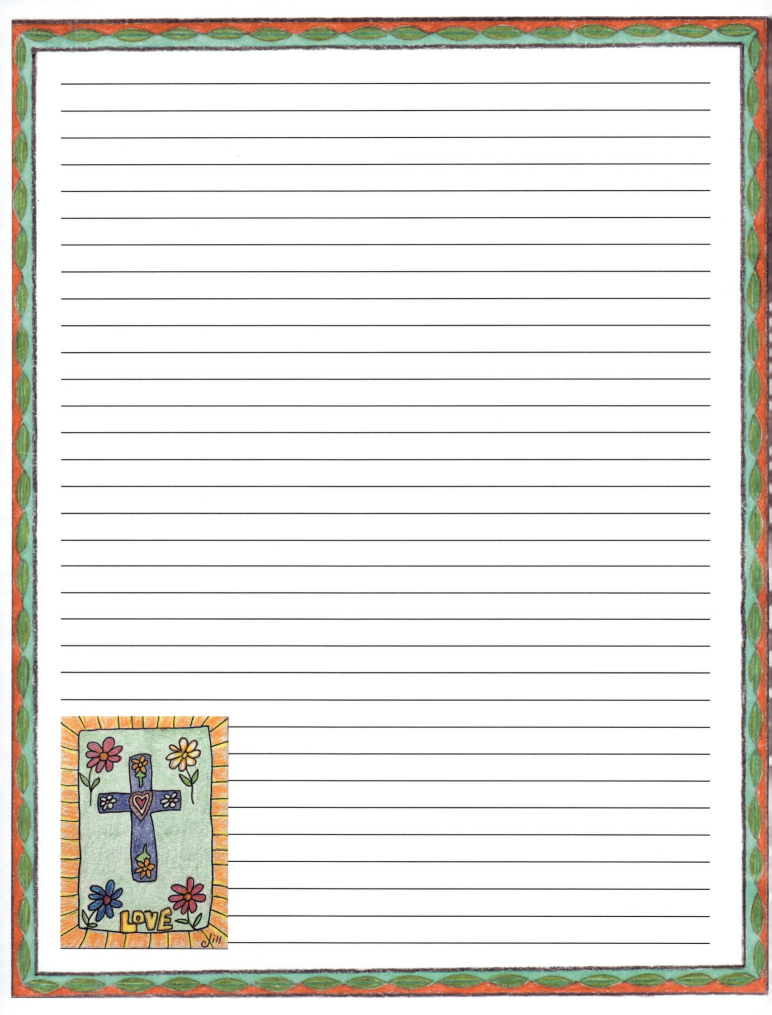

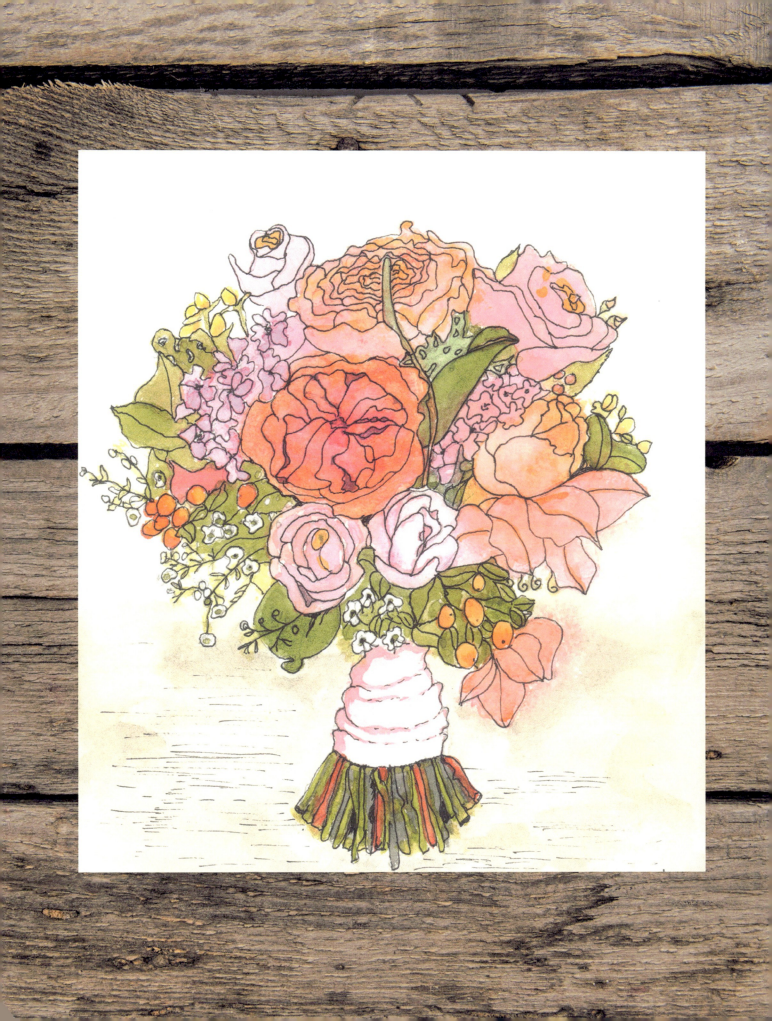

_____

_____

_____

_____

_____

_____

_____

_____

_____

_____

_____

_____

_____

_____

_____

_____

_____

_____

_____

_____

_____

_____

_____

_____

_____

_____

2 Corinthians 4:18

18 So we don't look at the troubles we can see now;
rather, we fix our gaze on things that cannot be
seen. For the things we see now will soon be gone,
but the things we cannot see will last forever.

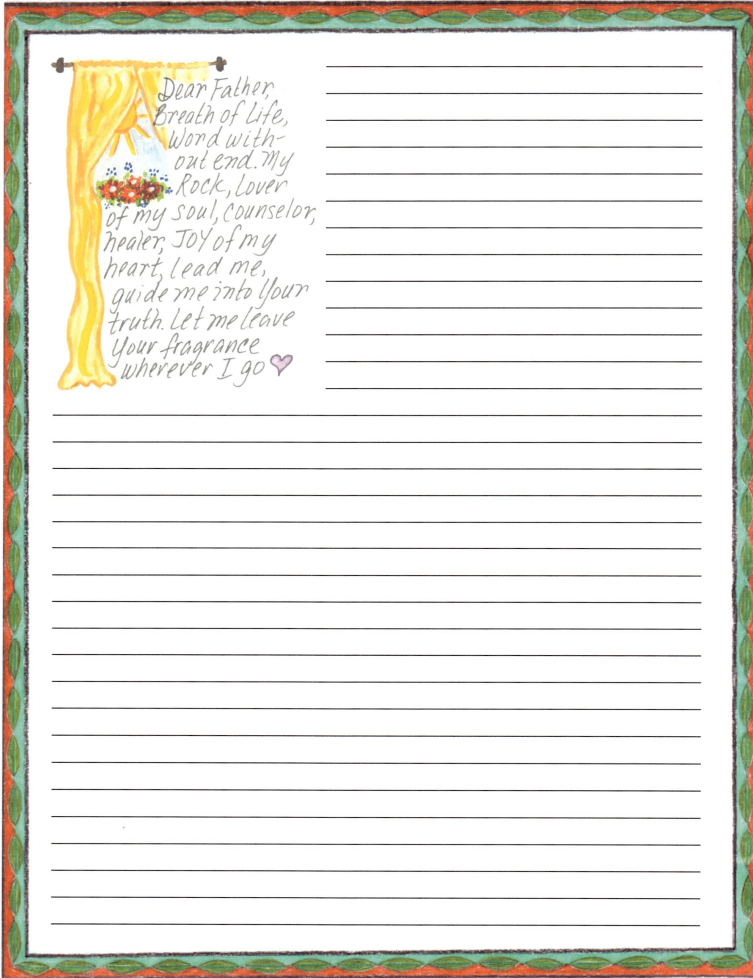

Dear Father,
Breath of Life,
Word with-
out end. My
Rock, Lover
of my soul, counselor,
healer, JOY of my
heart, lead me,
guide me into Your
truth. Let me leave
Your fragrance
wherever I go

'Freed,' You Ask?

Yes, 'Freed' from the burden of the wieght of your sin. You confess, "Jesus I can't bear my life anymore on my own. I don't know what to do. Please help me. I have made so many mistakes and hurt those I love." God will take your burdens and give you rest. He will help you make better decisions, one day at a time. Read His words and learn His ways, one day at a time. Jesus already was the sacrifice for all of your sins when He died on the cross. So all you have to do is ask and know that you are forgiven, made new and 'Freed'.

I John 5:14

14 And we are confident that He hears
us whenever we ask for anything that
pleases Him.

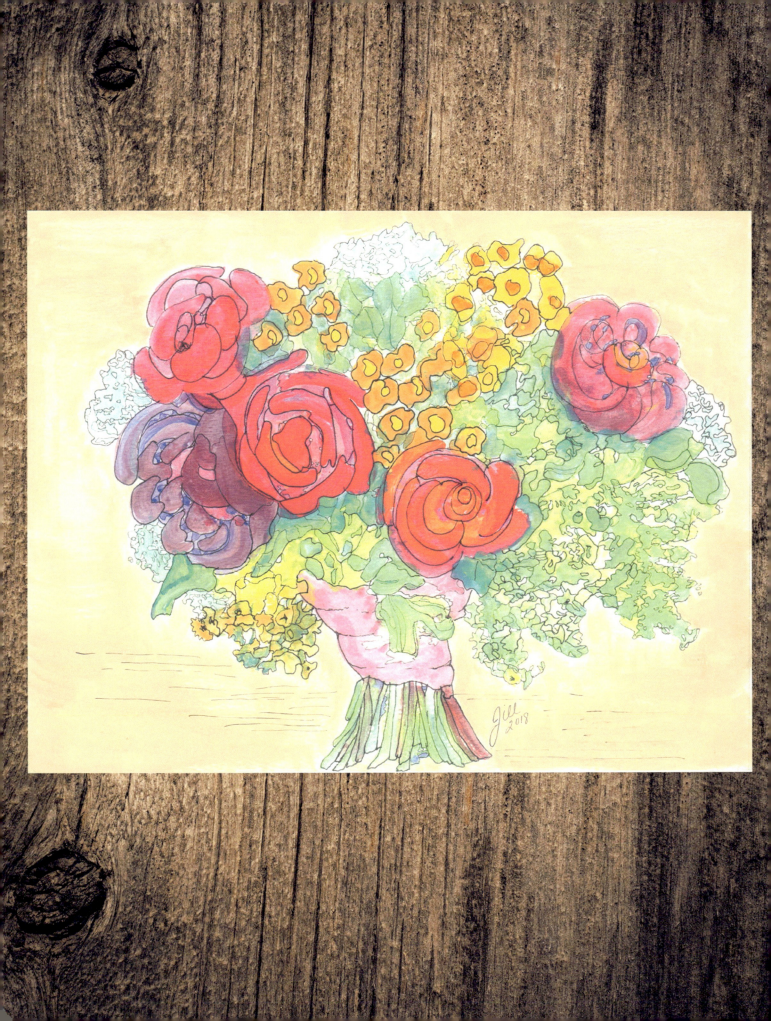

Those the lord has rescued will return. They will enter Zion with singing; everlasting Joy will crown their heads. Gladness and Joy will overtake them, and sorrow and sighing will flee away.

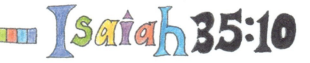

JOY

\joi \ noun

1. darkness dispelled.

2. the light of everlasting life lit up in the soul.

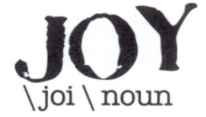

Alleluia!

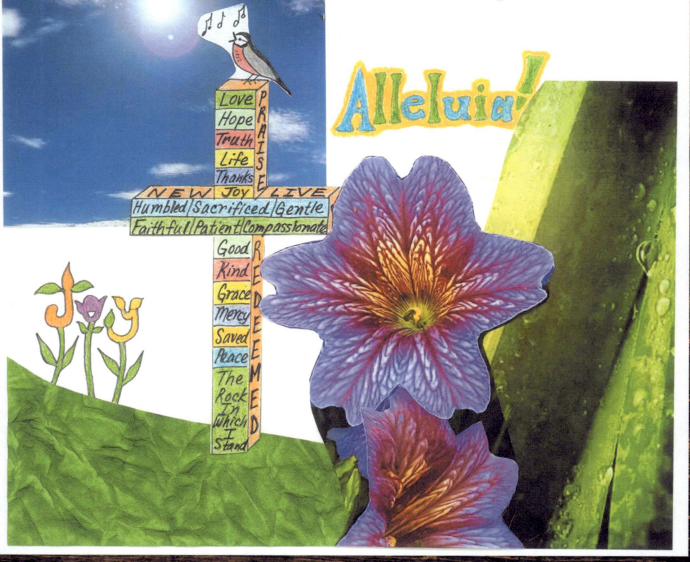

_____
_____
_____
_____
_____
_____
_____
_____
_____
_____
_____
_____
_____
_____
_____
_____
_____
_____
_____
_____
_____
_____
_____
_____
_____
_____
_____
_____

Psalm 62:5-8

5 Let all that I am wait quietly before God, for my hope is in Him. 6 He alone is my rock and my salvation, my fortress where I will not be shaken. 7 My victory and honor come from God alone. He is my refuge, a rock where no enemy can reach me. 8 O my people, trust in Him at all times. Pour out your heart to Him, for God is our refuge.

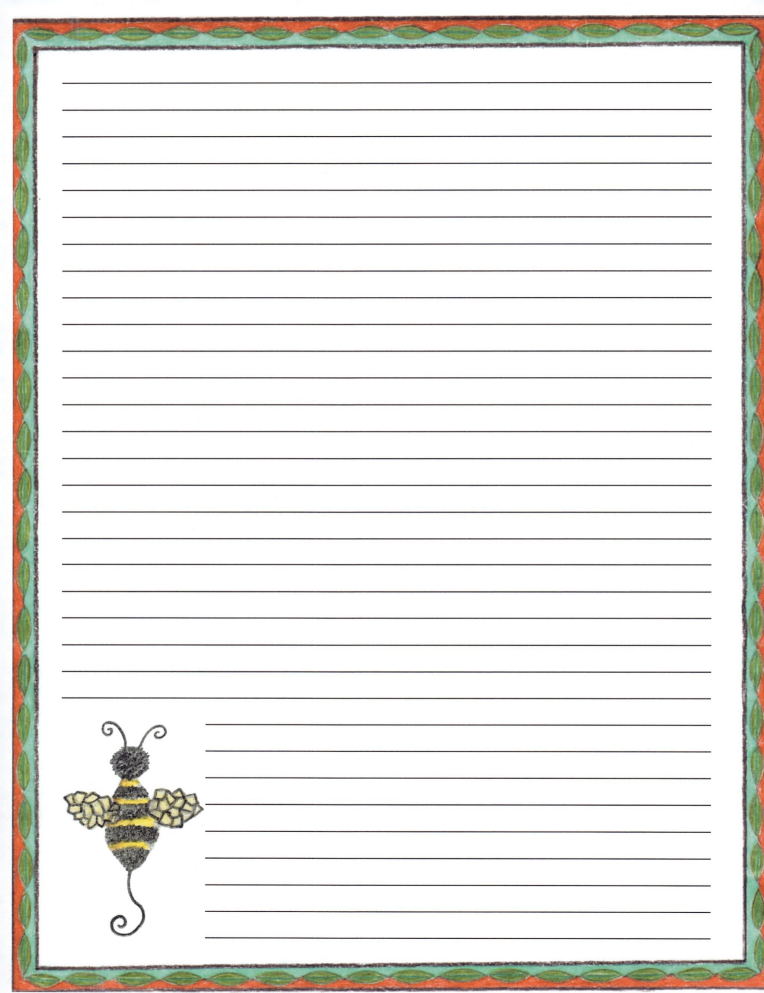

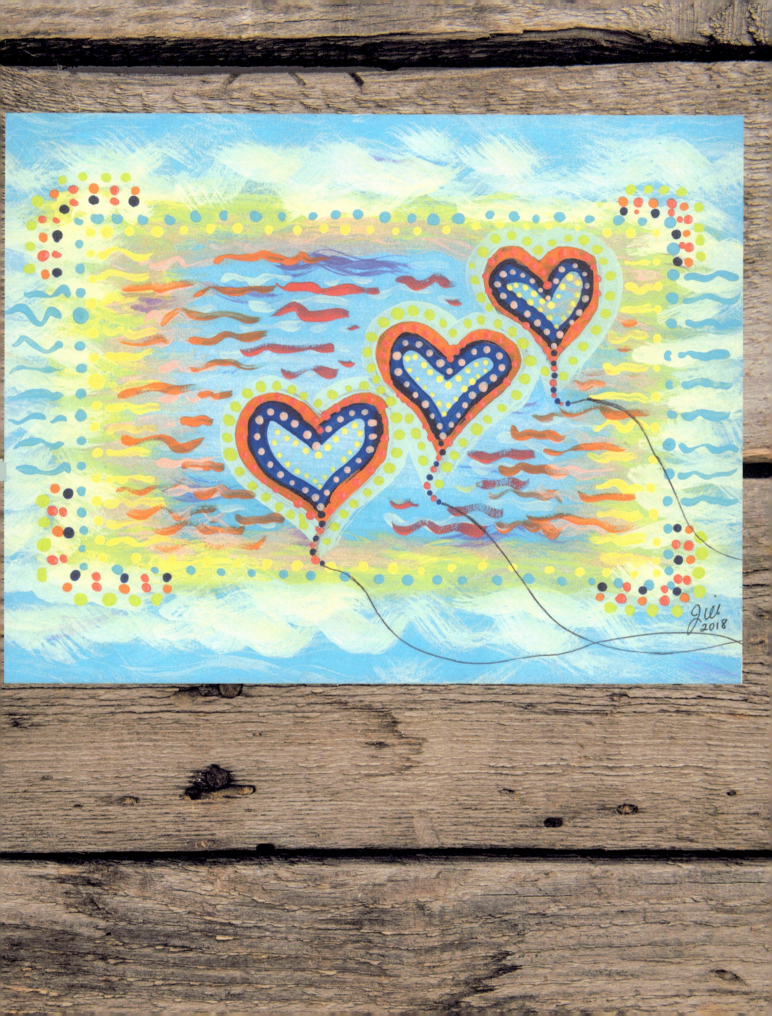

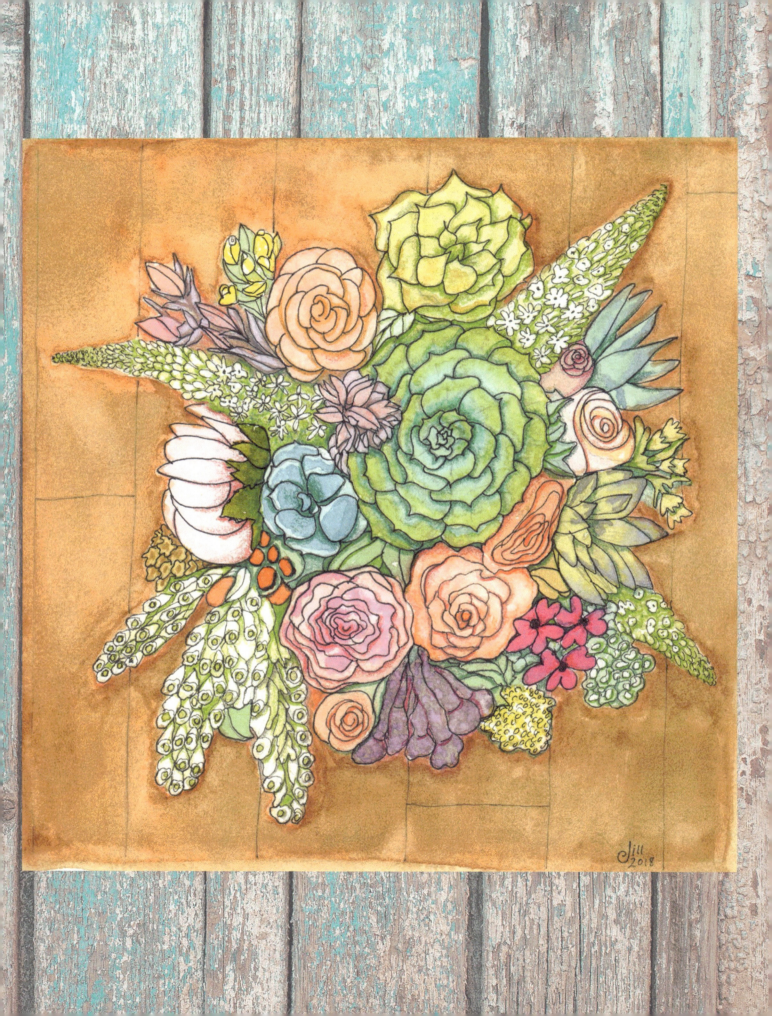

_____
_____
_____
_____
_____
_____
_____
_____
_____
_____
_____
_____
_____
_____
_____
_____
_____
_____
_____
_____
_____
_____
_____
_____
_____
_____
_____
_____

Proverbs 16:3
Commit your actions
to the Lord
and your plans will succeed.

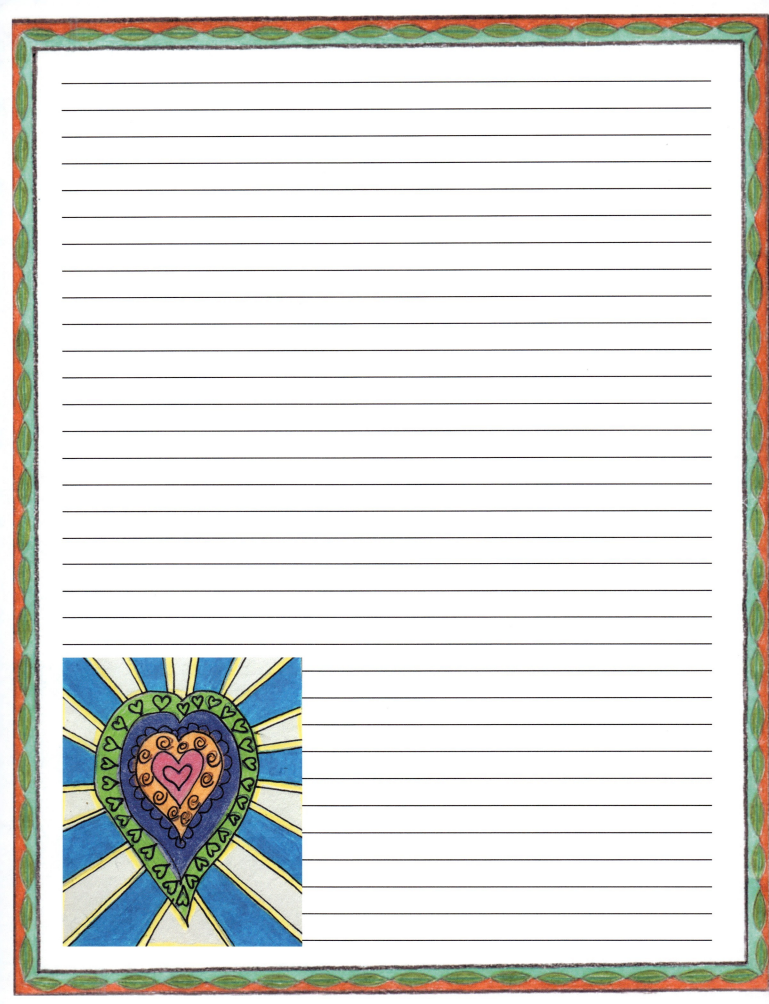

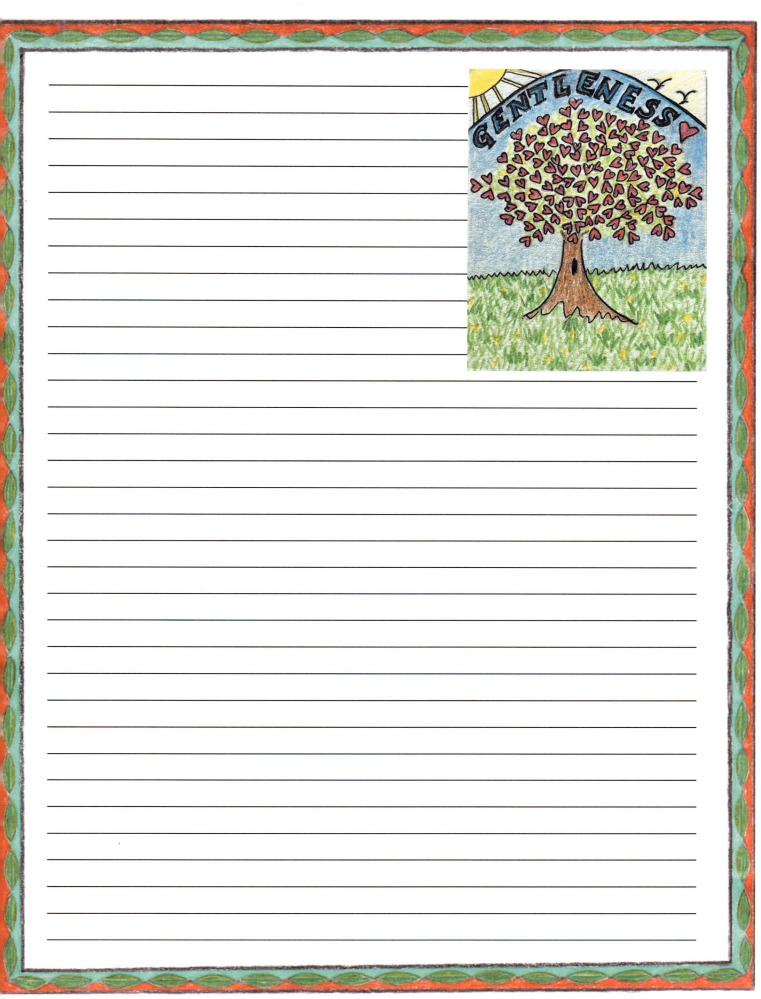

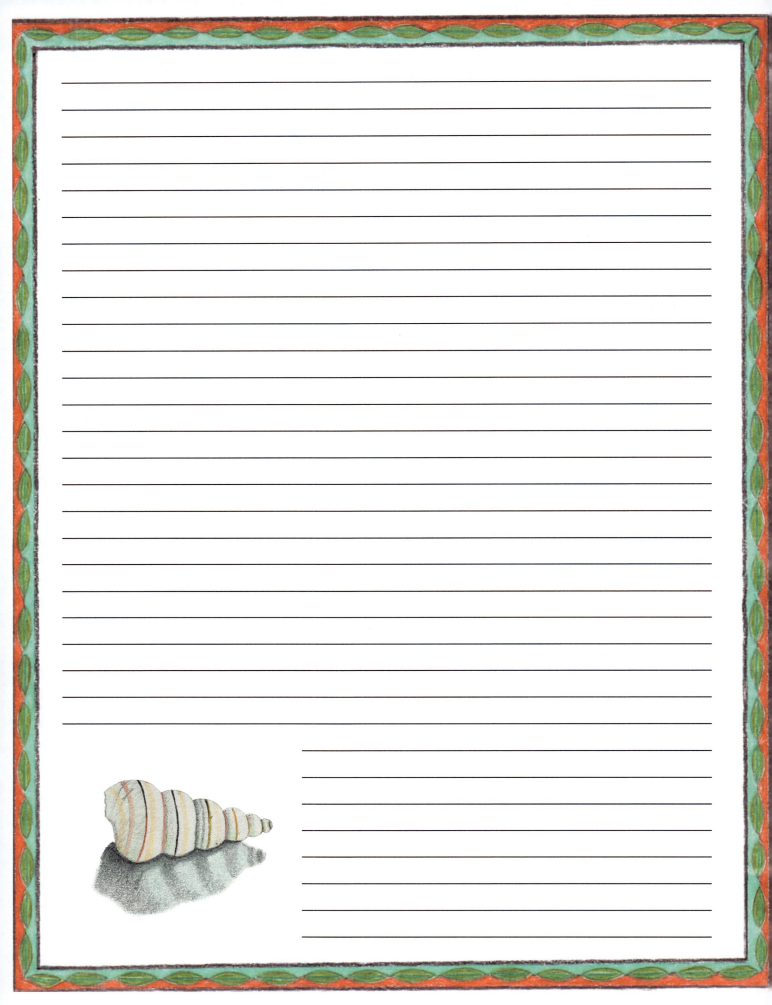

PSALM 63:1

"O GOD, YOU ARE MY GOD. EARNESTLY I SEEK YOU, MY SOUL THIRSTS FOR YOU, MY BODY LONGS FOR YOU, IN A DRY AND WEARY LAND WHERE THERE IS NO WATER."

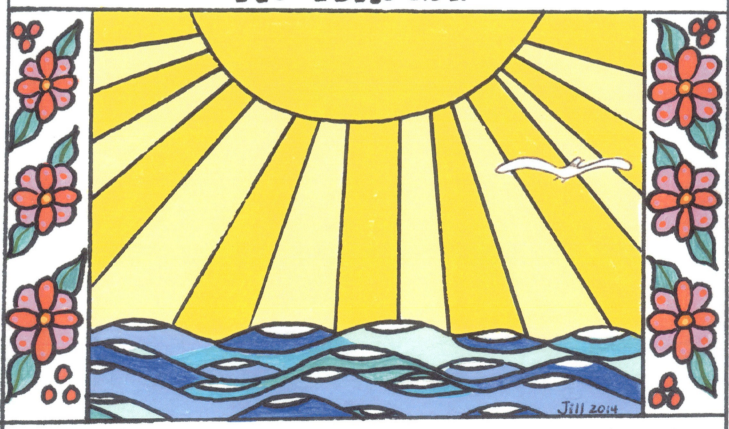

Jill 2014

SO I LOOKED FOR YOU IN THE SANCTUARY

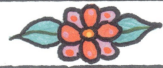

Father in Heaven,

Thank You for meeting me here as I draw close to You. In my daily time with You, You have given me so much hope and wisdom. You want a relationship with me and I am so thankful. Time spent with You is not in vain. It is time with You, my maker and lover of my soul, that gives me purpose in life. You want to hear about my hopes and dreams. You want to hear about my difficulties and pain. You want to make a beautiful tapestry out of my messy life that will glorify You. Let me always be thankful that You care. Please give others the same hope that You have given me as I spend time with You. You, God are my greatest cheerleader and healer. Thank You for opening my eyes as I read Your word. You give me wisdom and understanding into who You are and how much You want to help me. Grow me up and let Your light shine out of all my brokenness. Let me praise You to show You how much I love You. You love me right where I am, and right where I am I love you back. You are my best friend and You make my heart smile.

I come to you through Jesus' Name, Amen

_____

_____

_____

_____

_____

_____

_____

_____

_____

_____

_____

_____

_____

_____

_____

_____

_____

_____

_____

_____

_____

_____

_____

_____

_____

_____

_____

_____

_____

Lamentations 3:23-24

23 Great is His faithfulness;

His mercies begin afresh each morning.

24 I say to myself, "The Lord is my inheritance;

therefore, I will hope in Him!"

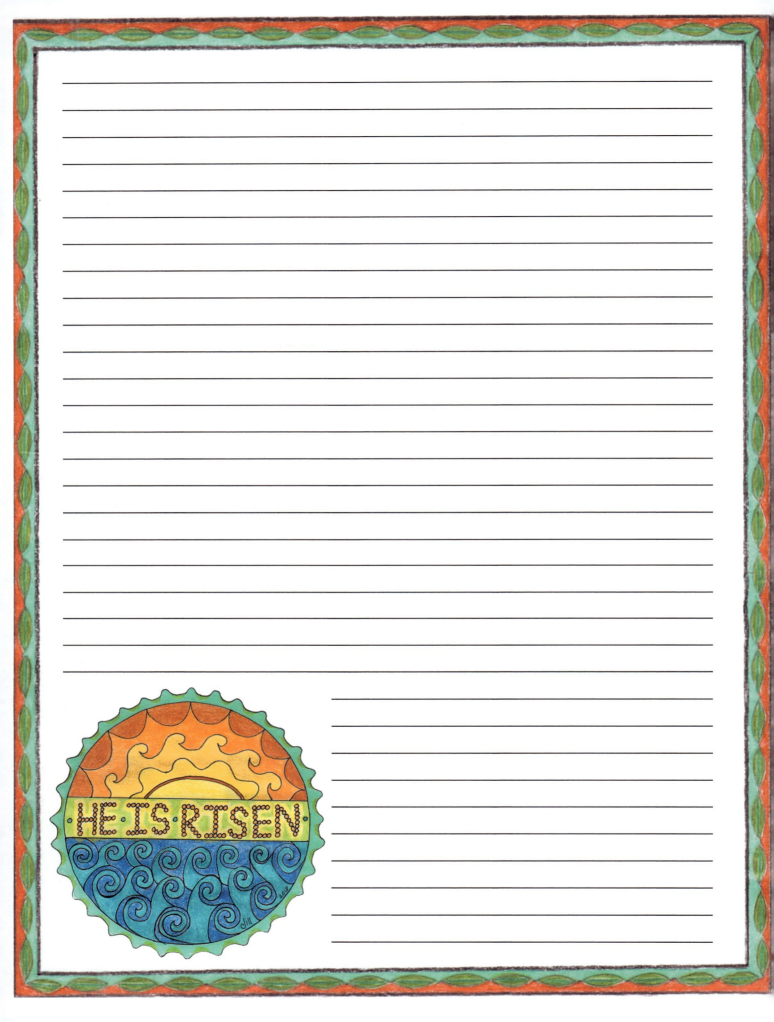

Praise Him!

My God, my Lord, my King, I praise You because You are good and I want You to know that I love You. My JOY comes from You. There is no one that even comes close to deserving our praise. You are light, and truth, Creator of beauty and goodness. You made all of creation: the mountains, the beaches, the turquoise waters, the fish, the birds, the flowers, and the sky. You made my two precious cats Callum and Runner. You made color and light. You made human life with Your very breath. You made the moon the sun and the stars and You control them. You are love and compassion. You, our God our King sent Jesus here to sacrifice Himself for the forgiveness of our sins, so that we could come and live with You one day. Jesus defeated death for us while we were still sinners. Your love is so beyond what we know in our small minds. I am in awe of You. I love You and humbly receive Your underserved gift of forgiveness, mercy, and grace. I will spend time with You and love You as much as I can as You teach me and love me and reveal Yourself to me.

Thank You, Father for adopting me, and loving me into your family.

In Your Son Jesus' Name, Amen

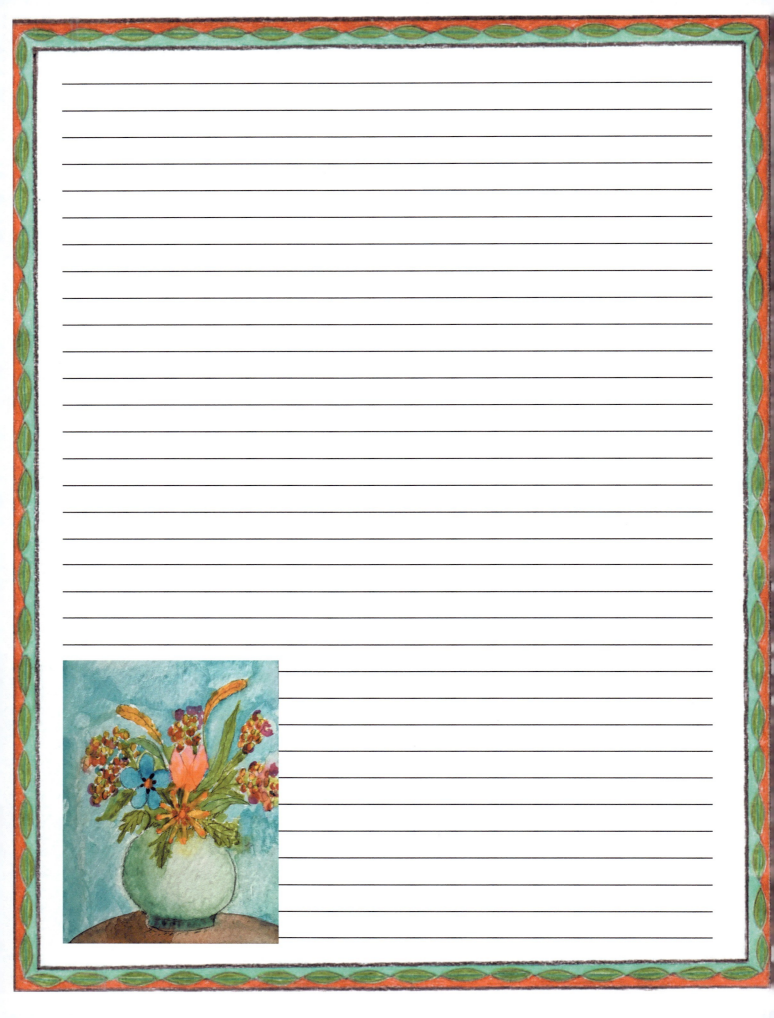

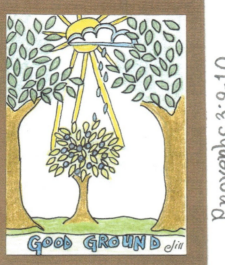

Good Ground

Be the good soil Mark 4

Proverbs 3:9-10

Honor the LORD with your wealth and with the best part of everything you produce. Then he will fill your barns with grain, and your vats will overflow with good wine.

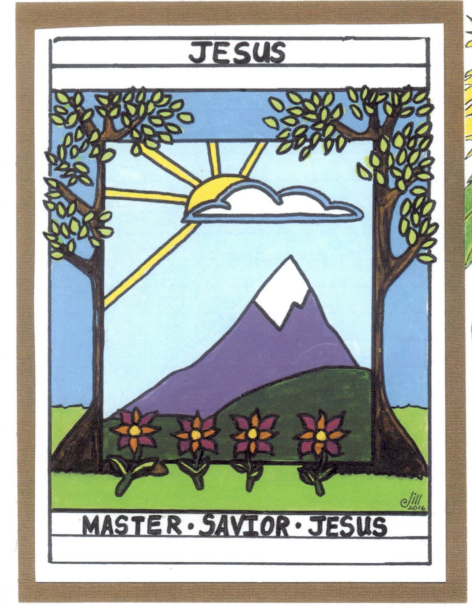

JESUS

MASTER · SAVIOR · JESUS

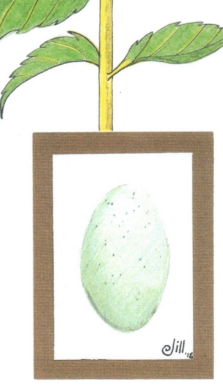

_____
_____
_____
_____
_____
_____
_____
_____
_____
_____
_____
_____
_____
_____
_____
_____
_____
_____
_____
_____
_____
_____
_____
_____
_____
_____
_____
_____
_____

2 Corinthians 4:16-18

16 That is why we never give up. Though our bodies are dying, our spirits are being renewed everyday. 17 For our present troubles are small and won't last very long. Yet they produce for us a glory that vastly outweighs them and will last forever! 18 So we don't look at the troubles we can see now; rather, we fix our gaze on the things that cannot be seen. For the things we see now will soon be gone, but the things we cannot see will last forever.

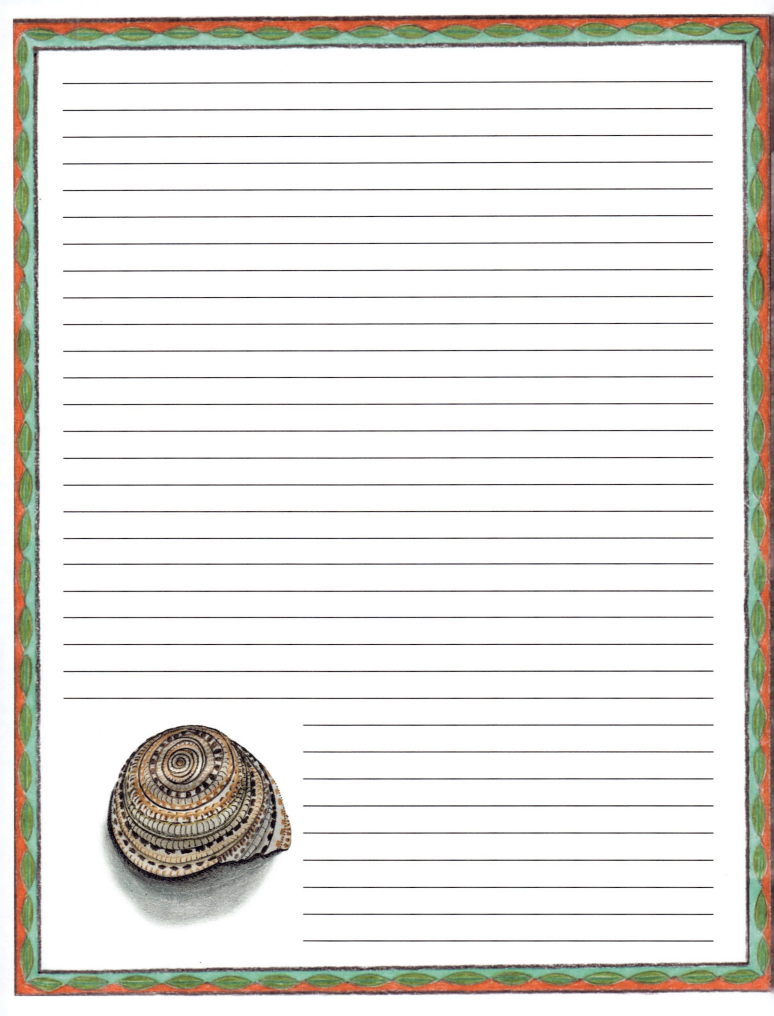

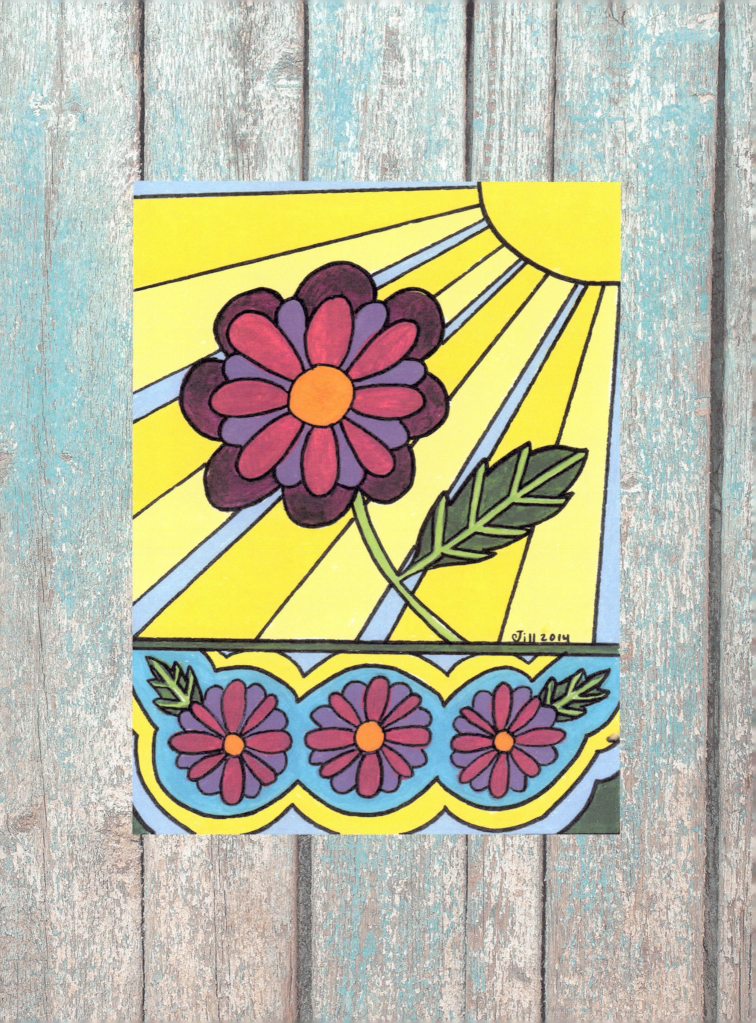

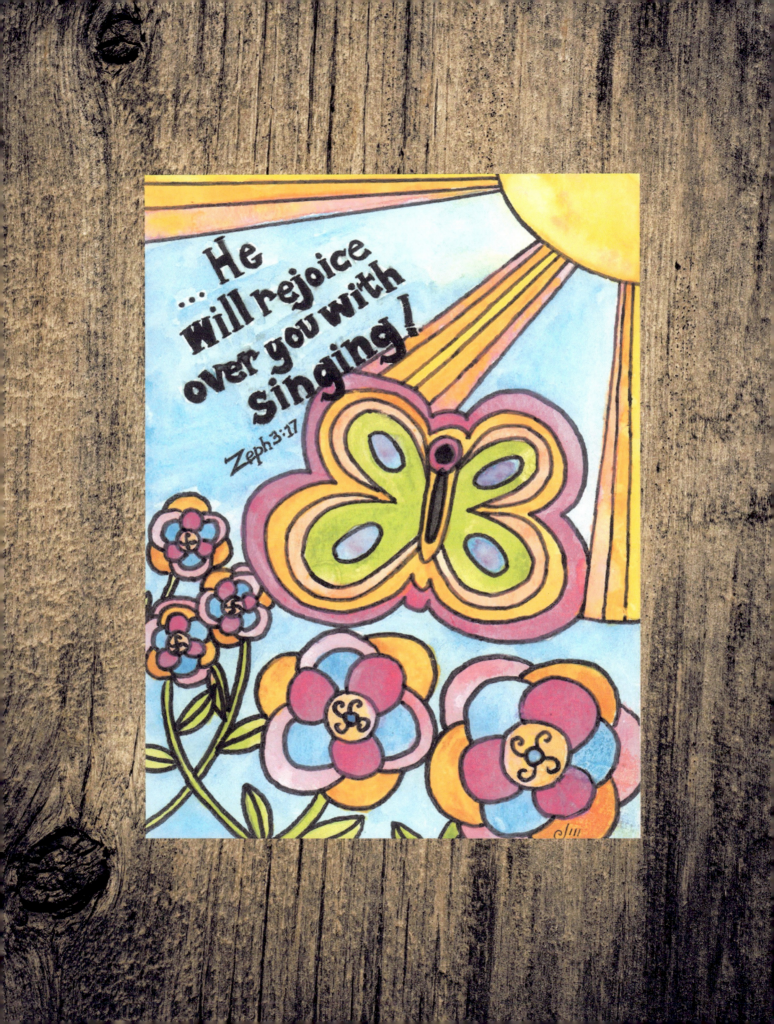

Psalm 9:1-2

1 I will praise You, Lord, with all my heart;

I will tell all of the marvelous things You have done.

2 I will be filled with JOY because of You.

I will sing praises to Your Name, O Most High.

Isaiah 33:2
2 But Lord, be merciful to us
for we have waited for You.
Be our strong arm each day
and our salvation in times of trouble.

Let God Grow You Up

🌼 Spend time with God. You will have more wisdom. God's wisdom, not what man says wisdom is.

🌼 You will start praying for people. People you love and people you never cared for.

🌼 Tell God a funny story that happened to you and laugh with Him.

🌼 Tell God about a choice you have to make and that you don't know what to do.

🌼 Or sometimes just be quiet and let His Word come to you and let it heal you.

🌼

Jeremiah 17:14
Oh Lord, if You heal me, I will be truly healed; if You save me, I will be truly saved. My praises are for you alone.

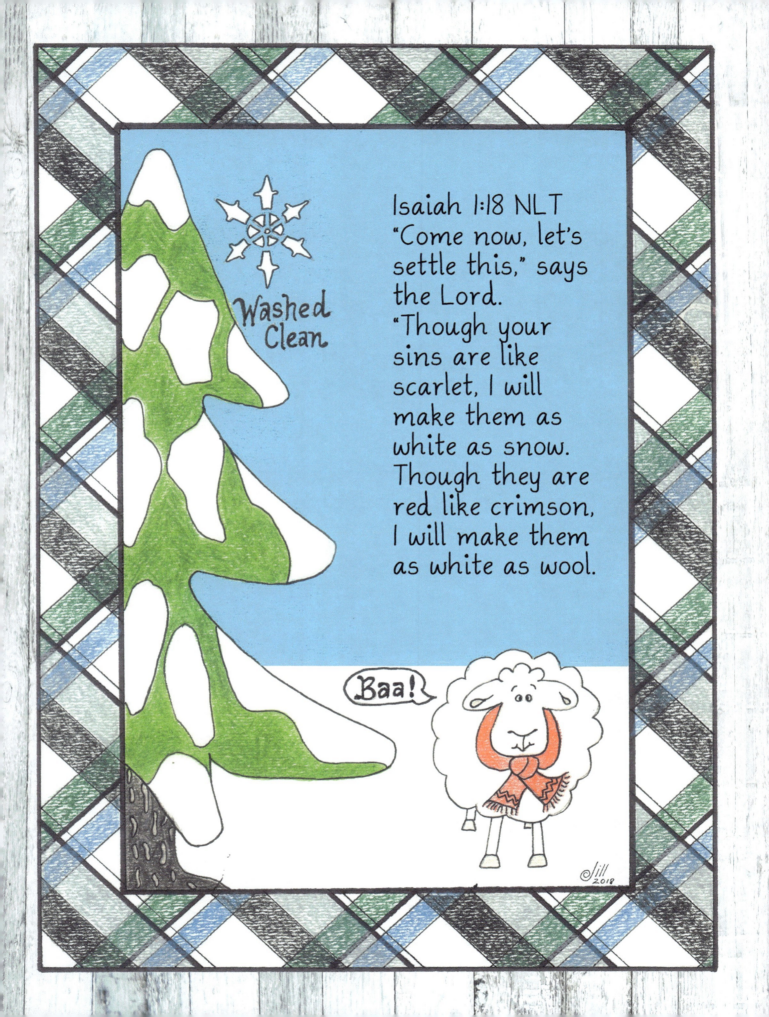

_____

_____

_____

_____

_____

_____

_____

_____

_____

_____

_____

_____

_____

_____

_____

_____

_____

_____

_____

_____

_____

_____

_____

_____

_____

_____

_____

_____

_____

Psalm 19:1
The heavens proclaim the glory of God.
The skies display His craftmanship.

Psalm 141:3
3 Take control of what I say
O Lord,
and guard my lips.

_____
_____
_____
_____
_____
_____
_____
_____
_____
_____
_____
_____
_____
_____
_____
_____
_____
_____
_____
_____
_____
_____
_____
_____
_____
_____
_____

Hebrews 10:23

23 Let us hold tightly without wavering to the
hope we affirm, for God can be trusted to
keep His promise.

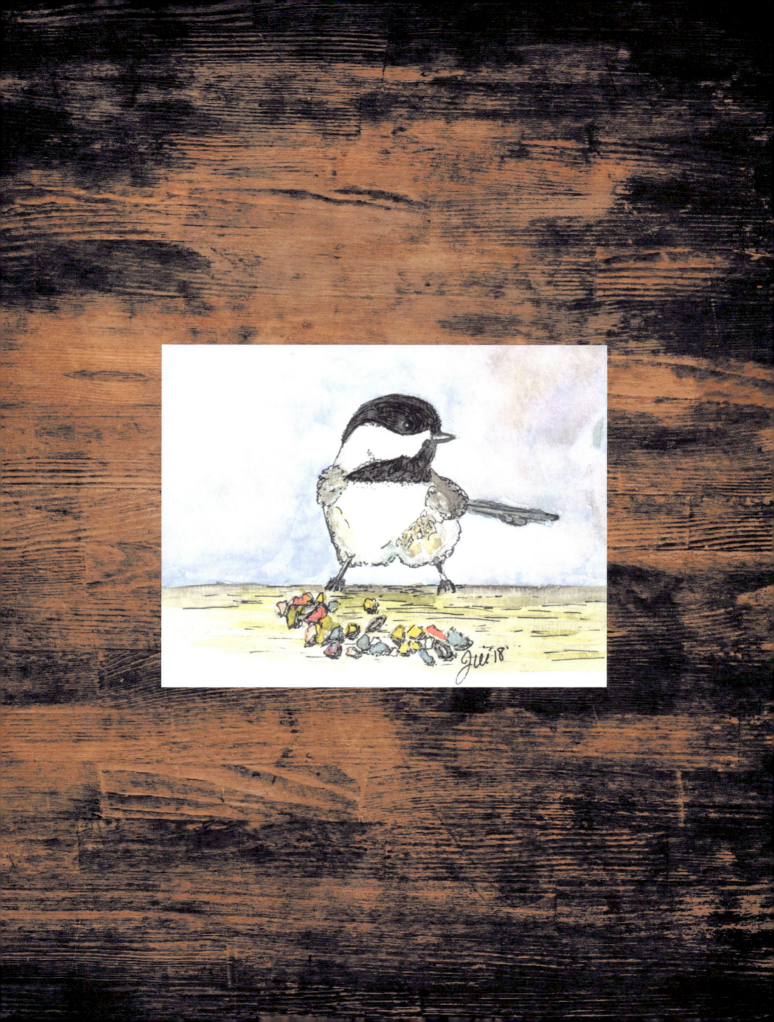

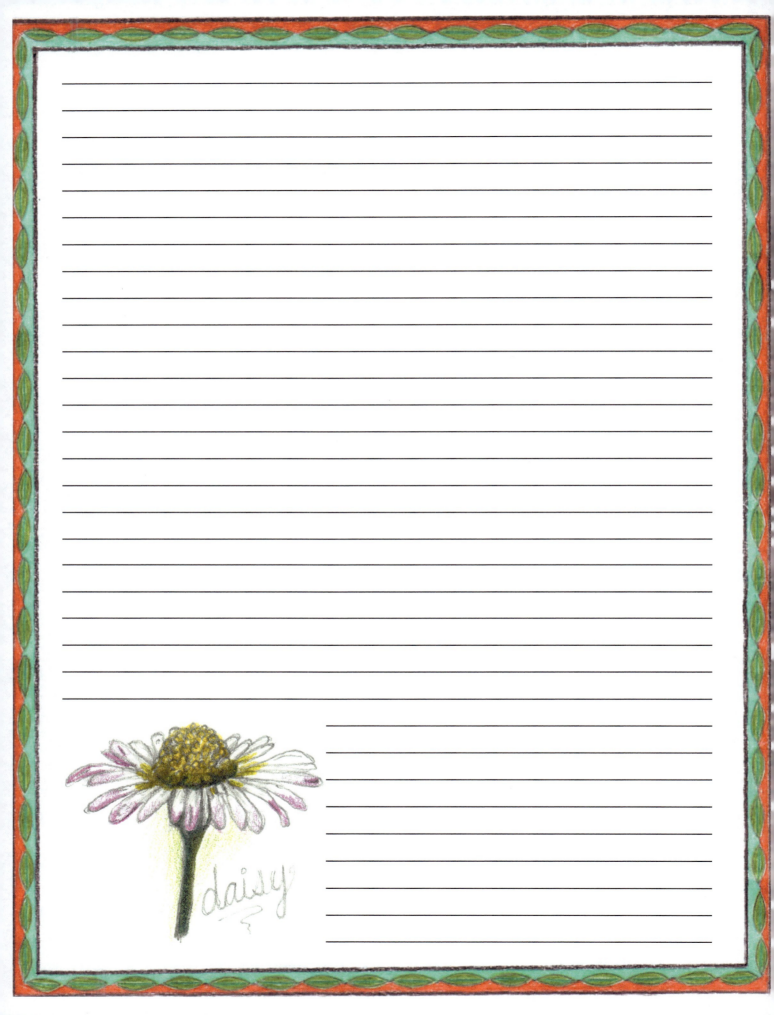

daisy

_____
_____
_____
_____
_____
_____
_____
_____
_____
_____
_____
_____
_____
_____
_____
_____
_____
_____
_____
_____
_____
_____
_____
_____
_____

Genesis 2:7
Then the Lord God formed the man
from the dust of the ground. He
breathed the breath of life into the
man's nostrils, and the man became
a living person.

Hello my friend,

My name is Jill Glorioso. I live in Maryland with my husband Nick and my son Cameron. I have attended Calvary Chapel of Baltimore for more than 22 years. Pastor Rick and his wife Tara are like another set of parents to me and have taught me biblically how to live my life as a follower of Jesus.

I have always been creative, finding satisfaction in making art to share JOY. So, combining two of my favorite things, art & Jesus, and spreading God's word has become my passion. Although I am a self-taught artist, I hope that what I have created lets you explore more ways to connect with your perfect Father in Heaven. I didn't make this a devotional, because I want you to find God's path in your own way. You decide what book in the Bible to start reading. You tell Him all about your life and let Him become your most important counselor and healer, friend, and confidant. Make Him first priority in your life and know that He will protect you and watch over you. He will share in your JOY and nudge you when you start to make a detour off His path. He is a good, good Father.

Love,

Your friend and Sister in Christ,

Jill

Printed in the United States
By Bookmasters